Goldy The little Mermaid
Book 1

HELP TRAIN YOUR CHILDREN'S IMAGINATION

Introduction

For many parents, curling up with a book for a bedtime story with their kid is a daily ritual. For others, it is the perfect time to spend time with their children after a busy day, and for some, it is something they should do but are not entirely sure why. Discover these benefits of bedtime stories for kids.

Sharpen their brains

Research shows that one of the greatest benefit of interacting with children, including reading to them stories, is that children learn a great deal of things- from improved logic skills to lowering their stress levels. Bedtime stories rewire the brain of a child and quicken their mastery of language. Their vocabulary repertoire is expanded and their listening and oral communication skills enhanced.

Enhance creativity and Stimulate imagination

If you are a good storyteller, then you should teleport your kid to a different realm- from reality to fantasy for the child to learn the difference between these two. This will enhance and stimulate his imagination.

Emotion development

The kid will learn to experience different emotions while empathizing with the characters of the story. The common emotions of sadness, happiness and anger may be encountered and he will learn to control these in real life.

Content

7 Tips to Help Ignite Your Child's Imagination

Imagination, often the concept we associate with joy, whimsy, and play, is just as easily involving cognitive capability, logical reasoning, and mental stability. The process the brain goes through when utilizing make-believe notions is a mixture of curiosity, adrenaline, and the practicing of creativity and exploration of different ideas previously unreached. Doing so exercises several parts of the adolescent mind, and will be reflected upon in the future, by means of open-mindedness, reason, and the ability to fathom abstractions above and beyond that of the average mind.

By incorporating these tips and activities into the lifestyles of both you and your child, your pudgy genius will not only be more mentally efficient, but happier and more capable overall.

1.   Ask Boggling Questions

Parents tend to underestimate the span of their child's intelligence, restraining their capacity. Ask questions that are "out of the box", for instance, "what do you think that toad is thinking?" or "how come the clouds are floating?" Questions that you wouldn't normally consider completely sane, probably absurd to the outside world, can be awe-inspiring and full of wonder to your child, opening doors of imagination and invention in their minds. In addition, try to respond to their answers with "why do you think that is?" or "how can you tell?", thereby teaching them that questions are meant to be explored, and ideas full of possibility. Most importantly, never allow your child to say "I don't know". Teach them that your questions have no right answer, as long as they make you think.

2.   Keep Questions Open-ended

Steer clear of words such as "wrong" or "try again", which will force children to believe that questions can only have one answer, with strict guidelines and a sole truth. They will later apply this mantra to their everyday behavior, and think in a more linear format, essentially restricting their minds and ideas.

3.   Ask "what if?"

What if trees could move? What if you your teacher were an ogre? What if giraffes could talk? Let your child explore things beyond the dimensions of reality, and allow them to conceive concepts far and wide.

4.   Tell Stories

Pictures and imagery are unimportant, even less effective than simply speaking a story to your child. Use different voices, adjectives, and hand gestures when speaking, allowing your child to fill in the blanks of the story, creating a sort of movie in their own heads. Unlike in TV, in stories, children do not have their visuals presented to them. Make these epic narratives engaging, and allow your child to add to the story. This will open the door to creative writing, as well as reading and extensive thought. It is so important to constantly exercise your child's mind, allowing it to be flexible and thrive in mentally straining instances in adulthood.

5. Create Art

Allow your child to openly explore their artistic talent. By letting your child draw, paint, or simply create the ideas in their minds, you are solidifying the concepts they invent, giving them meaning and allowing them to come to life. Even if their drawing capabilities are short of Mozart material, by creating art, your child will learn to express his or herself, perhaps opening up new areas of interest.

You can create hand puppets, form houses out of old packing boxes, or have fun with finger paints. The expanse of art is endlessly vast, and it's fine simply to explore its plains.

6. Encourage Openness

In addition to openness regarding the imagination, encourage trying new things. Whether this is varying foods, different school clubs, and even new friendships, your child can experience anything from an engaging hobby to understanding the conditions of friendship. Moreover, try not to overly shelter your child. Children who understand death at an early age will better cope with it in the future, and adolescents familiar with financial instability will learn from their parent's experiences and be more understanding and compassionate toward adversity. Of course, there is a period in childhood when not to be too open, just keep in mind that hiding everything from your child is not realistic nor healthy.

7.   Leave Room for Growth

A flower doesn't bloom under watch, and a child's imagination cannot grow in a cramped environment. Allow him or her space to explore the world. Let your child establish independence, while still maintaining the assurance of an adult figure, in case things go astray. It's often hard to let go of your child, and that's OK, however it's imperative to refrain from being overly invasive, as this will likely cause your child to become dependent and create a barricade between them and their full capacity.

Goldy The little Mermaid

In the deep ocean was a secret world. It was a world that was far away from the human eye; it was a world so beautiful that no human could ever imagine it. The mermaids who ruled this world lived in peace among themselves. They took care of the other sea creatures, as well.

The whole marine world was happy under the care of the mermaids. The mermaids followed a queen. This was the time for Queen Lily to rule. She was kind and just. She fed her kingdom before herself. The queen was the most selfless queen in all of the ocean. Queen Lily had an adopted daughter - a baby mermaid who had been abandoned at the outskirts of the kingdom. The guards mermaids found her sleeping on a large oyster shell. They took her to the queen. The queen searched for months, but no one came to claim the child.

The queen had then thought to give her to a family who needed a child as beautiful and tender as her. But over the last couple of months Queen Lily had gotten very attached to the baby, hence she finally ended up adopting her herself. The baby was fair with red cheeks and pink lips. Her eyes were as deep of a green as the deepest sea. But it was her curly golden hair that caught everyone's breath. Her long, golden hair waved around her neck and curled around her ears and forehead. She was named Goldie. The whole ocean rejoiced on her naming day. Goldie found a new home and a mother to love her, and the queen got a gem of a daughter in return.

As Goldie grew up around the palace, she was a delight to be around. She was polite and greeted everyone who came her way. "Good morning guards, good morning mother, good morning kind guests, good morning chef, good morning coral gardener...." She made her mother chuckle every morning. The same went on at noon and night.

Goldie made many friends in the kingdom; everyone wanted to be her friend. Her pleasant nature was a gift to be around. Everyone from a 1 year old to an 80 year old mermaid enjoyed her company. Among them all, Goldie had a special friend - a friend she grew up with. She was a Yellow Box fish - a daughter of one of Queen Lily's court generals. Her name was Tira.

Tira and Goldie were inseparable from the moment they met. Tira was 5 years younger than Goldie, but was quite mature, and smarter than any sea animal Goldie had ever seen. Tira would be frank with Goldie. While the rest of the kingdom flattered her with their praises, Tira the Box fish spoke to her only the utter truth. This was why Goldie loved having Tira around all of the time.

One day Queen Lily was brushing Goldie's long, golden hair. She loved to groom her daughter. Goldie was now 15 years of age. She had grown to be tall and beautiful. As she groomed her, the queen took off her crown and placed it on Goldie's head.

"Mama, that is the Queens's Crown," said Goldie.

"And it looks so beautiful on you," said the queen, looking at Goldie.

"But I shouldn't wear it," said Goldie.
"One day you will be a queen, and you will have to wear it all day," said her mother.
Goldie was overjoyed; she knew she was the princess, but never dreamt of being a queen.
"Me, a queen??" she asked.

Her mother laughed at her innocence.
"Yes, my child; who else is suitable for it other than you?" asked the queen.

Goldie jumped out of her chair. She held her mother's arms and twirled with joy. She was so happy.

Tira swam into Goldie's room.
"Oh, I'm sorry, your highnesses! I didn't mean to disturb you. I'm here to see Goldie," said Tira.

"Come on in, Tira - there's no need for apologies, child," said the queen.

Goldie rushed to Tira. She lifted her friend and hugged her.

"Tira, my mom just said I'm going to be the queen one day!" gushed the overly happy Goldie.

"Congrats, Goldie!" said Tira, but she had always known that Goldie would be the next queen.

"Excuse me, ladies. I've got work to complete...." said the queen. "Goldie, would you mind...?"

"Oh, yes, Mama " said Goldie as she took off the crown and placed it on her mother's head. Tira bowed as the queen passed.

Goldie and Tira walked off to shop in the Aqua Market. Goldie met her friend, a mermaid named Eliza

"Good day, Eliza! How are you?" she greeted Eliza.

"Hi, Goldie. Hi, Tira." Eliza waved at them.

"You look beautiful, Goldie," complimented Eliza.

"Thanks. Guess what? I'm going to be the next queen!" said Goldie. It just slipped out of her, since that was all she was thinking about.

"Oh, that's wonderful.... Congratulations. Is it official?" said Eliza.

"Oh, no, no - just a word by the queen," Tira broke in.

"Oh. well, congrats, Goldie. You will be a wonderful queen. Goodbye now," Eliza left, wishing Goldie well.

"What was that?" asked Goldie in anger. "You cannot announce it to everyone in the ocean, Goldie. It is something your mother told you in private," said Tira.

"So what? She said I would be the queen. Why should I wait for it to be official? Why can't they know it right away?" Goldie did not understand why her friend was advising her to keep the matter private.

"Goldie, I'm sure everyone in the ocean wants you to be their next queen, but such matters are also dangerous to the wrong ears. When you are ready your mom will make it official to all the marine world," Tira tried to explain. "Are you jealous? Don't you want to see your friend become a queen?" Goldie retorted at Tira.

She knew it was a wrong thing to do, but something in her made her say it, and she did not want to take her words back. This made Tira furious at Goldie.

"Oh, you cannot be furious! I'm your future queen," flared Goldie. She brushed her golden hair in pride.

This made Tira lose her temper, so she turned and swam off. She needed to calm down. Box fish are known for their short temper. So she swam away from the heated situation. Even Goldie turned her back on her best friend and swam away.

This was not the first time they had fought; they always fought about petty matters, but always came back together within an hour's time, missing each other.

Before anybody wondered, the word about Goldie taking over the throne after Queen Lily was spread throughout the ocean.

Every mermaid, fish, and marine mammal was talking about the big news. The word was spread to other kingdoms as well.

Some were worried how such a young girl would take over the throne, others were worried that she is not a true blood to the throne; many wondered why they were not officially informed by the royal family and the news was got to them by the locals. Different people treated the news differently. But among all of the news was brought a silver lining.

There was a group of dangerous and ugly looking Goblin Sharks that Queen Lily had banished from her kingdom and also helped the neighboring kingdoms to banish. For years they had been looking for vengeance. The news of the queen being changed reached them. But like every rumor, they got a version that was over-exaggerated.

"I heard Queen Lily had given the throne to her golden haired daughter," said one of the Goblin Sharks to their leader.

The leader of the Goblin Shark was Sewer, who had been defeated on the battle by Queen Lily, still bore a long scar across his face from the battle. Sewer was extremely happy upon hearing the news.

"ATTACK!" he said at once.

"Right now?" asked his messenger.

"Yes, right away. Let them rejoice in the crowning of their new queeen. Everybody will be engaged in the event and no one will be expecting us. Also, there will be guests from all the ocean wide kingdoms. We will destroy them all at once. This is the right time to take revenge for what they did to us. We will destroy them all. No mermaid shall survive!" he growled out loud.

"Get all of the goblins ready. We are going to war now," commanded Sewer.

His messenger did as told. He swam deeply and got all the goblins from their hiding. They made the ocean bed their home. They had fresh food to eat. And they could not come out in the open. This was the punishment Queen Lily had given them. Goblin Sharks had lived along with the mermaids, but they always destroyed the peace. They were reckless and uncontrolled - so much that Sewer once tried to destroy the royal palace since then Queen Lily had put an end to their violence and banned them from all Ocean Kingdome.

Today Sewer and his sharks have set to take revenge. Little do they know this was just a rumor, and Queen Lily still ruled the oceans.

Back at the kingdom, Goldie went around the market on her own. Everybody she met congratulated her. This shocked Goldie; she did not expect her small talk with Eliza would create such an impact. She realized what Tira was trying to tell her.

"I should look for Tira and apologize," she thought.

Meanwhile, the queen's messenger came gushing into her court.

"Your highness! Your highness!" cried a messenger out loud.

The entire court was alarmed by such disturbance.

"Your highness.. The Goblins. They have gathered an army they are heading here. Sewer has declared a war against us," the messenger said in a hurry.

All of the members of the court broke out. There were quick decisions made. The army had to be made ready with the strongest animals. All of the civilians had to be taken to safety. They had just a few hours.

The best of the guards were at the entrance to stop the goblin army. The mid level guards were spread all over the kingdom. The new members in the guards were assigned to clear the city and keep the people safe. Goldie was tracked down and dragged back to the palace. Her mother had to be in the battle, just like before. Goldie said goodbye to her mother, and Tira was brought to Goldie. After hours of preparation, the Goblin Shark army reached the kingdom. Sewer, who was leading the army, was stunned to see the mermaid army ready to go against them. It was a fierce battle, but the Goblin Sharks had no chance against the mermaids, especially as Queen Lily was leading the army. Finally, after hours and hours of battle the Goblin Sharks gave up. Sewer was caught and jailed. It was too dangerous to exile the goblins again. Sewer admitted he came under the circumstances of the rumors that the throne was passed on to a new queen.

Queen Lily was speechless to hear this from him. How did the word spread so far?
The goblins were put away in cells for lifelong imprisonment.

Queen Lily once again saved the ocean.

Later that night, Goldie and Tira waited patiently in Goldie's room for the news about the battle. Queen Lily walked into her room. "Mom, you are all right!" Goldie rushed over and hugged her mom. Tears rolled down her eyes.

Queen Lily was happy for her safety, as well. Queen Lily asked Goldie and Tira about the rumors. They narrated how the war had started.

Goldie was speechless over how a small, lightly spoken word had created a battle in her kingdom.

She cried and cried... and her mother and Tira consoled her.

"It is ok to be enthusiastic, Goldie, my dear, but never speak a word without thinking. A small mistake causes a day long battle - just because a word was spoken out loud and carried out in so many different forms." "Nobody even realized who did it, but it's a total different story at the other end," explained her mother.

Goldie learned a very important lesson that day: Never to speak without thinking, and never to carry out rumors.

THE END.

ABOUT AUTHOR

Nona J. Fairfax.

Nona J. Fairfax is an accomplished storybook author that has a strong passion for writing when it comes to improving the lives of children. She has a strong sense of pride for her work, and continues to thrive for a more universal world that keeps children and families in the foremost front of her mind. Her life's work includes writing children's books that help to improve the parent-child relationship, bedtime stories, and smaller pieces of art. When she is not busy writing about improving the lives of children.

MY BEST SELLER ON AMAZON

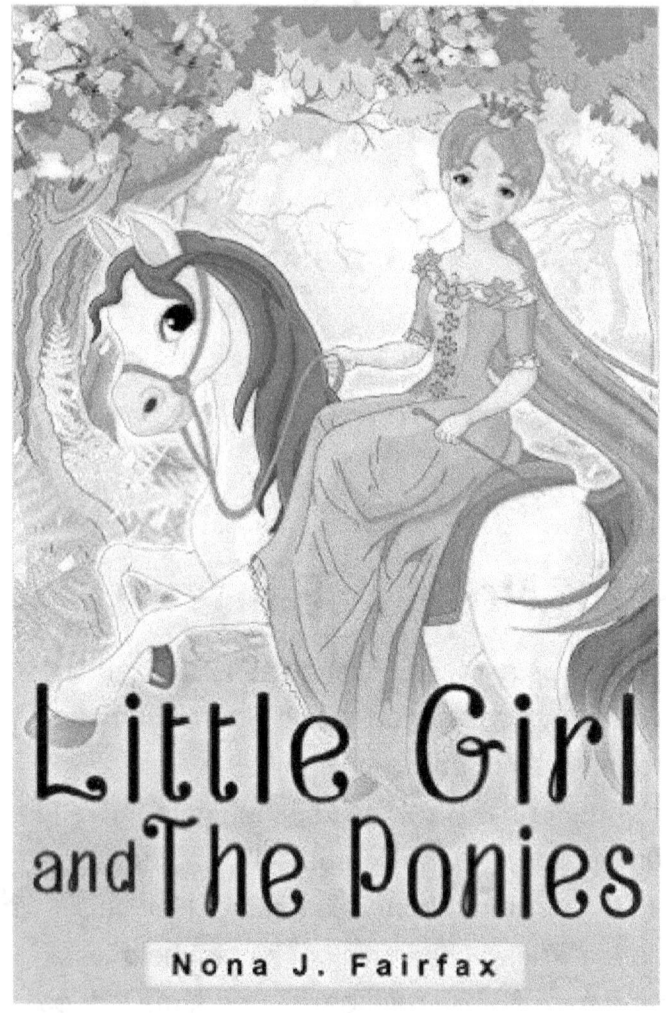

Little Girl and The Ponies

Nona J. Fairfax

Download on:
www.amazon.com/dp/B00S2V6Z1W

Download on:
www.amazon.com/dp/ B00Y5DC4MU

Download on:
www.amazon.com/dp/B00Z7CJI72

Download on:
www.amazon.com/dp/ B010EAB0JA

Download on:
www.amazon.com/dp/B010LP0TJU

The FAIRY PRINCESS and The Unicorn

NONA J. FAIRFAX

Download on:
www.amazon.com/dp/ B00WXI5HDM